OUR
GRE★T
STATES

D1310362

WHAT'S GREAT ABOUT
OHIO?

✳ Darice Bailer

LERNER PUBLICATIONS ✳ MINNEAPOLIS

CONTENTS

OHIO WELCOMES YOU! ✳ 4

Content Consultant: Thomas Sosnowski,
Professor of History, Kent State University

Lerner Publications Company
A division of Lerner Publishing Group, Inc.
241 First Avenue North
Minneapolis, MN 55401 USA

For reading levels and more information, look
up this title at www.lernerbooks.com.

Main body text set in ITC Franklin Gothic Std
Book Condensed 12/15.
Typeface provided by Adobe Systems.

Library of Congress Cataloging-in-Publication
Data

Bailer, Darice.
      What's great about Ohio / by Darice
Bailer.
        pages cm. — (Our great states)
      Audience: Grades K–3.
      ISBN 978-1-4677-3885-9 (lb : alk.
paper) — ISBN 978-1-4677-8515-0 (pb : alk.
paper) — ISBN 978-1-4677-8516-7 (eb pdf)
      1. Ohio—Juvenile literature. I. Title.
F491.3.B28 2015
977.1—dc23   2014043366

Manufactured in the United States of America
1 – PC – 7/15/15

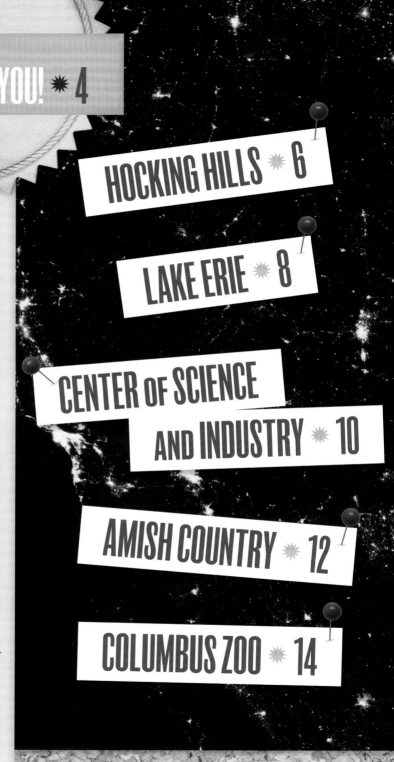

OHIO Welcomes You!

Say "Hi!" to Ohio! This state is packed with parks, museums, and tons of outdoor fun. Start your tour with a journey to Lake Erie. You can explore islands and waters. If you're looking for more adventure, the Roller Coaster Capital of the World is nearby. Hang on tight! Ohio has many exciting cities like Columbus and Cincinnati. There's so much to do and see in Ohio that it's hard to know where to start. Read on to learn all about Ohio's top ten places to visit.

Explore Ohio's parks and
all the places in between!
Just turn the page
to find out about the
BUCKEYE STATE. >

CANADA

Rattlesnake
Island

LAKE ERIE

South Bass
Island

Kelleys
Island

Toledo

Maumee River

Lorain   Cleveland

Parma   Cuyahoga
                River

Akron   Youngstown

PENNSYLVANIA

Campbell Hill
(1,550 feet/
472 m)   Canton

Great Miami River   N

Columbus

Dayton   Ohio River

Miles
0   10   30   50
0   40   80
Kilometers

Cincinnati

Ohio River

WEST
VIRGINIA

KENTUCKY

INDIANA

HOCKING HILLS

> Do you like hunting for buried treasure? Head to Hocking Peaks Adventure Park in southeastern Ohio. Use a compass to follow clues. Each clue will lead you to hidden treasure. If you can find every treasure chest, you'll earn a prize!

Then head over to Hocking Hills Canopy Tours. Try the Dragonfly adventure. It's a zip line course created just for kids. The course has three swinging rope bridges. Put on a harness and fly through the air. Enjoy the ride high above the ground! Before you leave, check out Hocking Hills State Park just down the road. The park is full of exciting natural wonders. The Rock House is a tunnel-like cave with giant natural windows. From inside, you can hear waterfalls thundering over cliffs.

Follow a compass to buried treasure at Hocking Peaks Adventure Park!

Fly through the air at the Dragonfly adventure, part of Hocking Hills Canopy Tours.

LAKE ERIE

> Next, travel north to visit Lake Erie. In Sandusky, you can climb on a ferry headed for South Bass Island. When you land, check out Perry's Victory and International Peace Memorial across from the dock. The giant column is 352 feet (107 meters) tall! Scale the lighthouse across the island. When you've reached the top, look across Lake Erie. Can you find Rattlesnake Island? It is just 2 miles (3.2 kilometers) away. Some say rattlesnakes once slithered all over it! And nearby Kelleys Island has ancient stone carvings made by American Indians.

Sail back to the mainland and visit the city of Sandusky. It's the Roller Coaster Capital of the World! At Cedar Point, you can soar, twist, and dive on one of the amusement park's sixteen roller coasters. The Top Thrill Dragster goes from 0 to 120 miles (193 km) per hour in fewer than four seconds! And the Iron Dragon roller coaster will swoop you low over the lagoon. Cool off on Thunder Canyon. It's a whitewater rafting adventure right in the park. Dress to get wet!

THE WAR OF 1812

During the War of 1812, US Navy commander Oliver Hazard Perry led his American sailors to victory against the British navy in the Battle of Lake Erie. In 1912, one hundred years later, Ohio began building Perry's Victory and International Peace Memorial to remember the battle. The memorial celebrates peace between the United States, the United Kingdom, and Canada, which had been a colony of the United Kingdom.

How far can you see from the top of Cedar Point's roller coasters?

CENTER OF SCIENCE AND INDUSTRY

> Explore the fun side of science at the Center of Science and Industry (COSI) in Columbus. Test your science knowledge in hands-on labs just for kids. Then learn to ride a unicycle on a wire high in the air. The weighted unicycle won't let you fall off! When your feet are back on the ground, head over to WOSU@COSI. It's a TV and radio studio set up for kids. As you explore the museum, you may also see and pet live animals, such as a bearded dragon.

The COSI Planetarium is the largest in Ohio. You can see the whole galaxy just by looking up into the 60-foot (18 m) dome. Some of the planetarium's shows explore underwater volcanoes and the inside of the human body.

In COSI's Gadgets exhibit you can take apart appliances to see how they work. Turn on a laser and watch it bounce between mirrors and prisms. Then try lifting yourself off the ground with the pulley machine. The Gadgets exhibit even has dancing robots!

You've probably never unicycled this high before!

OHIOAN ASTRONAUTS

Famous astronauts John Glenn and Neil Armstrong were born in Ohio. In 1962, John Glenn became the first American astronaut to fly around Earth. In 1969, Neil Armstrong became the first man to walk on the moon.

FIRST MAN ON THE MOON

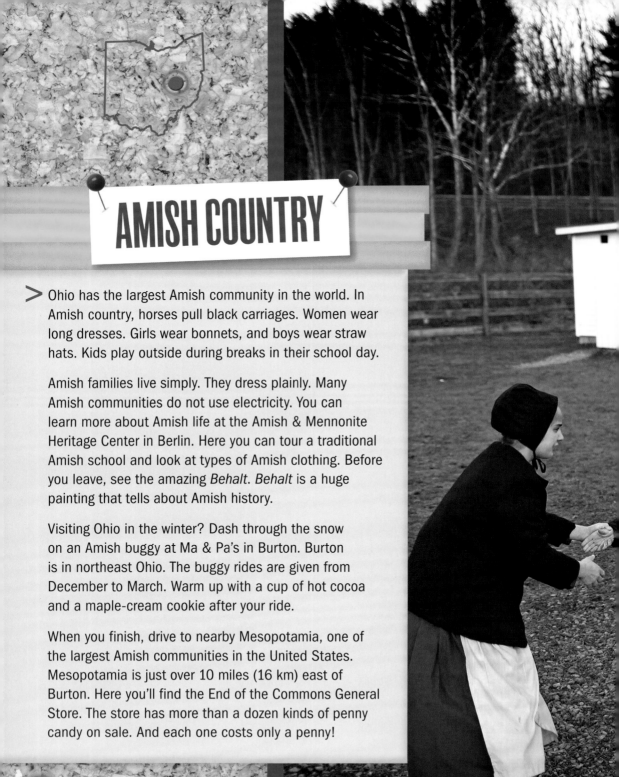

AMISH COUNTRY

> Ohio has the largest Amish community in the world. In Amish country, horses pull black carriages. Women wear long dresses. Girls wear bonnets, and boys wear straw hats. Kids play outside during breaks in their school day.

Amish families live simply. They dress plainly. Many Amish communities do not use electricity. You can learn more about Amish life at the Amish & Mennonite Heritage Center in Berlin. Here you can tour a traditional Amish school and look at types of Amish clothing. Before you leave, see the amazing *Behalt*. *Behalt* is a huge painting that tells about Amish history.

Visiting Ohio in the winter? Dash through the snow on an Amish buggy at Ma & Pa's in Burton. Burton is in northeast Ohio. The buggy rides are given from December to March. Warm up with a cup of hot cocoa and a maple-cream cookie after your ride.

When you finish, drive to nearby Mesopotamia, one of the largest Amish communities in the United States. Mesopotamia is just over 10 miles (16 km) east of Burton. Here you'll find the End of the Commons General Store. The store has more than a dozen kinds of penny candy on sale. And each one costs only a penny!

THE AMISH

The Amish began moving from Europe to the United States in the early 1700s. They wanted to practice their religion freely. Many settled in Pennsylvania. These days, large Amish communities exist in Ohio, Indiana, Iowa, Illinois, and Kansas. In 2014, more than 290,000 Amish lived in North America.

The biggest horse and buggy in the world sits outside the End of the Commons General Store in Mesopotamia.

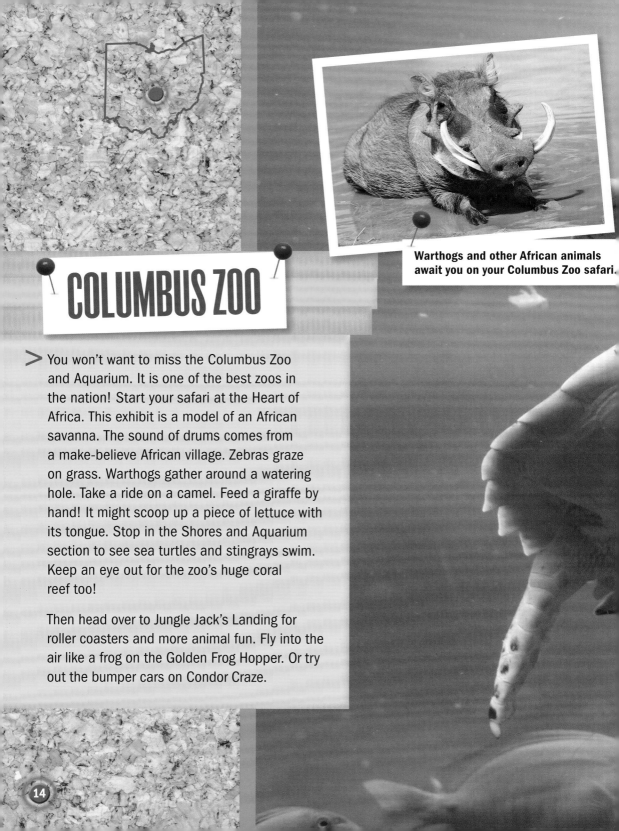

COLUMBUS ZOO

Warthogs and other African animals await you on your Columbus Zoo safari.

> You won't want to miss the Columbus Zoo and Aquarium. It is one of the best zoos in the nation! Start your safari at the Heart of Africa. This exhibit is a model of an African savanna. The sound of drums comes from a make-believe African village. Zebras graze on grass. Warthogs gather around a watering hole. Take a ride on a camel. Feed a giraffe by hand! It might scoop up a piece of lettuce with its tongue. Stop in the Shores and Aquarium section to see sea turtles and stingrays swim. Keep an eye out for the zoo's huge coral reef too!

Then head over to Jungle Jack's Landing for roller coasters and more animal fun. Fly into the air like a frog on the Golden Frog Hopper. Or try out the bumper cars on Condor Craze.

Bumper cars are just one of many fun rides at the zoo.

Can you hit the bull's-eye at the state fair's archery range?

OHIO STATE FAIR

> The Ohio State Fair in Columbus is one of the largest state fairs in the United States. This fair is packed with things to do. There are pony rides, a Ferris wheel, a giant slide, and pig races. There's even a watermelon-seed spitting contest! Stop by the Youth Center for tons of kid activities. Watch crazy science experiments with liquid nitrogen or build a rocket. Then check out model trains made out of Lego pieces! One ride, the Giant Slide, is 144 feet (44 m) long! Want to catch a fish or shoot an arrow? Fishing, kayaking, and archery are all free. Take a break with a comedy or magic show. They happen every day.

Don't leave without trying the famous fair food. Try roasted corn on the cob or a roast beef sundae. Want something sweet? A banana dog is a fried banana with peanut butter and chocolate sauce. Yum!

You won't have any trouble finding something good to eat at the Ohio State Fair.

CUYAHOGA VALLEY

> The Cuyahoga Valley is known for its beautiful trees, waterfalls, and rolling hills. Explore the area with a ride on the Cuyahoga Valley Scenic Railroad. This train chugs along the Cuyahoga River through Cuyahoga Valley National Park. Buy your ticket at an antique train depot. The train's bell clangs as the engine pulls into the station. Grab a window seat for the best view. Once you're on your way, look for animals in the park. Can you spot a bald eagle or a blue heron?

In November and December, elves read the classic picture book *The Polar Express*. The train transforms into the magical train from the story. Wear your pajamas for this magical trip to the North Pole to fetch Santa Claus. Wrap your hands around a warm cup of cocoa as you enjoy the tale.

AMERICAN INDIANS

Cuyahoga is an Iroquoian word that means crooked river. The Iroquois and other American Indians lived on the land before it became Ohio. Ancient people left behind many traces of their lives in Ohio. Some American Indians built great mounds, such as the Serpent Mound in southern Ohio.

If you're lucky, you'll spot wildlife from the window on your Cuyahoga Valley Scenic Railroad journey.

FLYING IN DAYTON

> Want to learn more about airplanes? Head to Dayton to learn about the history of flight! First, stop by the Dayton Aviation Heritage National Historical Park. Learn about Wilbur and Orville Wright. They invented the first airplane! See the bicycle shop where the brothers dreamed up their plane. Then look at life-size models of the planes they built.

Next, head over to the National Museum of the United States Air Force. It's located at Wright-Patterson Air Force Base just east of Dayton. This site has fun scavenger hunts in store for you! On your hunt, you'll see hundreds of aircraft. There are fighter jets and presidential planes. Did you know that many airplanes are named after birds, bugs, or other animals? What would you name a plane? Before you leave, explore the open fighter jet. You can sit in the cockpit. Try the controls and imagine you're flying high above the clouds.

See artifacts and photos from the bicycle shop where the Wright brothers invented their airplane.

FATHERS OF FLIGHT

The inventors of the first airplane, Orville and Wilbur Wright, were born in Ohio. Their plane was called the Wright Flyer. In 1903, Orville flew the machine for the first time. It flew for twelve seconds.

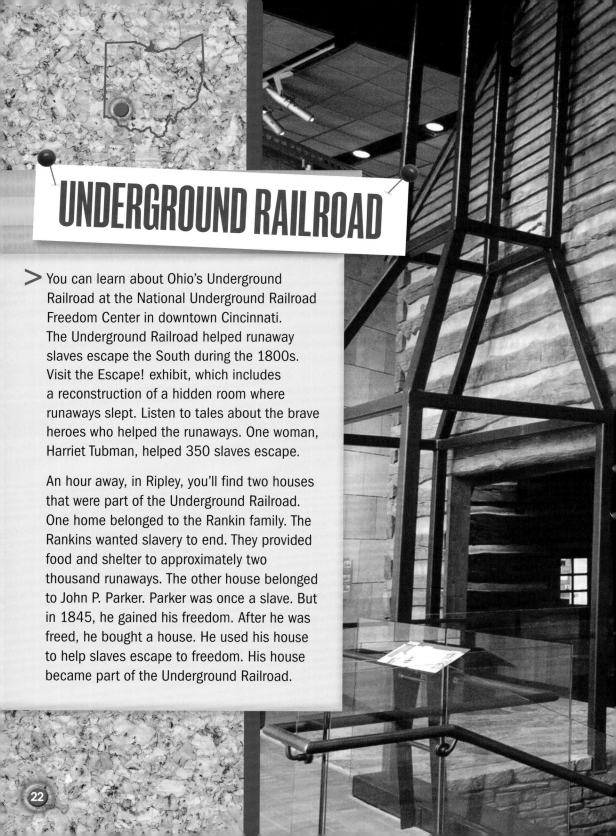

UNDERGROUND RAILROAD

> You can learn about Ohio's Underground Railroad at the National Underground Railroad Freedom Center in downtown Cincinnati. The Underground Railroad helped runaway slaves escape the South during the 1800s. Visit the Escape! exhibit, which includes a reconstruction of a hidden room where runaways slept. Listen to tales about the brave heroes who helped the runaways. One woman, Harriet Tubman, helped 350 slaves escape.

An hour away, in Ripley, you'll find two houses that were part of the Underground Railroad. One home belonged to the Rankin family. The Rankins wanted slavery to end. They provided food and shelter to approximately two thousand runaways. The other house belonged to John P. Parker. Parker was once a slave. But in 1845, he gained his freedom. After he was freed, he bought a house. He used his house to help slaves escape to freedom. His house became part of the Underground Railroad.

This artistic depiction of African American life at the National Underground Railroad Freedom Center took thirty years to finish.

What will you learn about Harriet Tubman's amazing life at the National Underground Railroad Freedom Center?

KINGS ISLAND

> Kings Island is the largest amusement and water park in the Midwest. It's located in Mason, about a half-hour northeast of Cincinnati. Ride to the top of a model of the Eiffel Tower. You'll be able to see the whole park.

You and your family can compete at bumper cars. The tube ride at White Water Canyon is sure to leave you soaked.

Don't miss Dinosaurs Alive! It's the world's largest animatronic dinosaur park. You can see and learn about more than sixty-five life-sized dinosaurs. Hear stories about dinosaur discoveries. The dinosaurs thrash their long tails and roar.

Then pretend you're a paleontologist. Get your shovel ready and go on a dinosaur dig. A skeleton of a dinosaur is hidden in the sand. What dinosaur is it? Find out, junior paleontologist.

Adventure awaits at Kings Island.

YOUR TOP TEN!

You just read about ten great things to see and do in Ohio. If you were planning a trip to Ohio, what would be on your top ten list? What animals or sights would you like to see? What Ohio activities sound most exciting? Write down your top ten choices. You can turn your choices into a book just like this one. Search the Internet or magazines for pictures. Print or cut them out to fill the pages. Or draw your own.

OHIO BY MAP

> MAP KEY

⭐ Capital city

◯ City

◯ Point of interest

▲ Highest elevation

—··— International border

—·— State border

—— Cuyahoga Valley Scenic Railroad

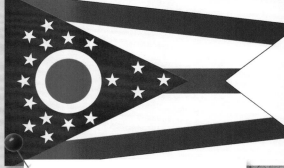

Visit www.lerneresource.com to learn more about the state flag of Ohio.

MICHIGAN

CANADA

LAKE ERIE

Rattlesnake Island

South Bass Island

Kelleys Island

Toledo

Maumee River

Cedar Point (Sandusky)

Lorain

Parma

NASA Glenn Visitor Center

Cleveland

End of the Commons General Store (Mesopotamia)

Ma & Pa's (Burton)

Akron

Cuyahoga River

Youngstown

Canton

N

Columbus Zoo and Aquarium

Ohio State Fair

Center of Science and Industry

Amish & Mennonite Heritage Center (Berlin)

Ohio River

PENNSYLVANIA

Campbell Hill (1,550 feet/ 472 m)

Great Miami River

Columbus

Dayton Aviation Heritage National Historical Park

National Museum of the United States Air Force

Hocking Hills State Park

Hocking Peaks Adventure Park

Dayton

Logan

Kings Island (Mason)

WEST VIRGINIA

Cincinnati

Serpent Mound (Peebles)

National Underground Railroad Freedom Center

Ohio River

Miles
0   10   30   50
0   40   80
Kilometers

INDIANA

KENTUCKY

OHIO FACTS

NICKNAME: The Buckeye State

SONG: "Beautiful Ohio" by Ballard McDonald, Wilbert McBride, and Mary Earl

MOTTO: "With God, All Things Are Possible"

> **FLOWER:** red carnation

TREE: buckeye

> **BIRD:** cardinal

ANIMAL: white-tailed deer

FOOD: tomato

DATE AND RANK OF STATEHOOD: March 1, 1803; the 17th state

> **CAPITAL:** Columbus

AREA: 44,825 square miles (116,096 sq. km)

AVERAGE JANUARY TEMPERATURE: 28°F (–2°C)

AVERAGE JULY TEMPERATURE: 73°F (23°C)

POPULATION AND RANK: 11,570,808; 7th (2013)

MAJOR CITIES AND POPULATIONS: Columbus (822,553), Cleveland (390,113), Cincinnati (297,517), Toledo (282,313), Akron (198,100)

NUMBER OF US CONGRESS MEMBERS: 16 representatives, 2 senators

NUMBER OF ELECTORAL VOTES: 18

NATURAL RESOURCES: clay, coal, gravel, natural gas, petroleum, salt, sand, sandstone

> **AGRICULTURAL PRODUCTS:** apples, eggs, hogs, milk, soybeans, tomatoes

MANUFACTURED GOODS: cars, chemicals, machinery, metals, paint, parts for cars and trucks, soap, steel, trucks, varnish

STATE HOLIDAYS AND CELEBRATIONS: Ohio Freedom Festival, Ohio State Fair

GLOSSARY

animatronic: a puppet, a model, or a statue that is moved by electronics and machinery

antique: something old or from an earlier period of time

commander: the leader of a group of people in the armed forces

liquid nitrogen: a very cold chemical that quickly freezes whatever it touches

memorial: something that honors the memory of a person or an event

prism: an object made of glass or plastic that separates any light that passes through it into different colors

safari: a trip taken to hunt or observe animals

savanna: a flat, grassy plain in a tropical area without trees

LERNER

SOURCE™

Expand learning beyond the printed book. Download free, complementary educational resources for this book from our website, www.lernersource.com.

FURTHER INFORMATION

Center of Science and Industry
http://www.cosi.org/exhibits/cosi-classics
You won't want to miss a visit to COSI. Learn more about the amazing exhibits at the museum!

Levine, Susan Sachs. *Packard Takes Flight: A Bird's-Eye View of Columbus, Ohio*. Charleston, SC: History Press, 2010. Follow the adventure of a baby peregrine falcon as he tries to find his way home in Columbus.

Ohio.gov
http://ohio.gov/government/kids
This site's fun facts and activities will teach you about the state's government.

Ohio History Connection
http://www.ohiohistory.org/kid
Learn about exciting historic sites and activities around Ohio.

Rubini, Julie K. *Hidden Ohio*. Watertown, MA: Mackinac Island Press, 2009. Learn more about Ohio's history. Look for hidden pictures and discover fun things to do.

Schulz, Walter A. *Johnny Moore and the Wright Brothers' Flying Machine*. Minneapolis: Millbrook Press, 2011. Read about Johnny Moore, a young boy who helped the Wright brothers prepare for their historic flight.

INDEX

PHOTO ACKNOWLEDGMENTS

The images in this book are used with the permission of: © tankbmb/iStock/Thinkstock, p. 1; NASA, pp. 2–3; © American Spirit/Shutterstock Images, p. 4; © James Marvin Phelps/Shutterstock Images, p. 5 (top); © Laura Westlund/Independent Picture Service, pp. 5 (bottom), 27; © Michael Shake/Shutterstock Images, pp. 6–7; © BananaStock/Thinkstock, p. 6; © moodboard/Corbis, p. 7; © SF Photo/Shutterstock Images, pp. 8–9; © Everett Collection/Alamy, p. 9 (top); © D. MacDonald/Photri Images/Alamy, p. 9 (bottom); © Steven Saus CC 2.0, pp. 10–11; © Do the things you cannot do CC 2.0, p. 11 (top); © Zoltan Katona/Shutterstock Images, p. 11 (bottom); © Michael Francis McElroy/ZumaPress/Newscom, pp. 12–13; © Cindy Hopkins/Alamy, p. 13 (bottom); © North Wind Picture Archives/Alamy, p. 13 (top); © DrexRockman CC 3.0, pp. 14–15; © Stacey Ann Alberts/Shutterstock Images, p. 14; © Digital Vision/Photodisc/Thinkstock, p. 15; © marada CC 2.0, pp. 16–17; © IconArts/iStock/Thinkstock, p. 16; © Erica Cherup CC 2.0, p. 17; © E Photos CC 2.0, pp. 18–19; © Tom Till/Alamy, p. 18; © ScooperDigital/iStock/Thinkstock, p. 19; National Park Service, pp. 20–21; © Walter Bibikow/Danita Delimont Photography/Newscom, p. 21 (left); © Photos.com/Thinkstock, p. 21 (right); © Pablo Alcala/KRT/Newscom, pp. 22–23; © Phil Marty/MCT/Newscom, p. 23 (top); Library of Congress, p. 23 (bottom) (LC-DIG-ppmsca-02909); © Josué Goge CC 2.0, pp. 24–25; © Kenneth Sponsler/Shutterstock Images, p. 24 (top); © Family Fun/MCT/Newscom, p. 24 (bottom); © nicoolay/iStockphoto, p. 26; © vikiri/Shutterstock Images, p. 29 (top); © Doug Lemke/Shutterstock Images, p. 29 (middle left); © Zack Frank/Shutterstock Images, p. 29 (middle right); © Patryk Kosmider/Shutterstock Images, p. 29 (bottom).

Cover: © Adeliepenguin/Dreamstime.com (Cedar Point roller coaster); © Kenneth Sponsler/Shutterstock.com (Cuyahoga Valley Scenic Railroad); © Eric Albrecht/Getty Images (Amish buggy); © Laura Westlund/Independent Picture Service (map); © iStockphoto.com/fpm (seal); © iStockphoto.com/vicm (pushpins); © iStockphoto.com/benz190 (corkboard).